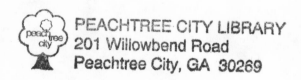

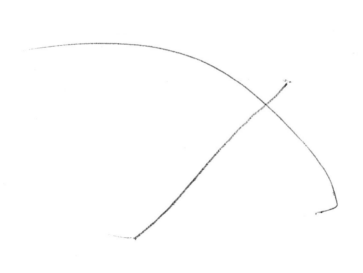

*Zebulon Montgomery Pike*

# THE WORLD'S GREAT EXPLORERS

## *Zebulon Pike*

By Susan Sinnott

CHILDRENS PRESS ®

CHICAGO

*Wooden monument erected in Sackets Harbor, New York, over the remains of Zebulon Pike. Sackets Harbor, on Lake Ontario, was a U.S. naval station during the War of 1812.*

Project Editor: Ann Heinrichs
Designer: Lindaanne Donohoe
Cover Art: Steven Gaston Dobson
Engraver: Liberty Photoengraving

**Library of Congress Cataloging-in-Publication Data**
Sinnott, Susan.
    Zebulon Pike/by Susan Sinnott.
        p.    cm. — (The World's great explorers.)
    Includes bibliographical references and index.
    Summary: Describes the adventures and travels of the army officer who explored the upper Mississippi, Great Plains, and Colorado area before the War of 1812.
    ISBN 0-516-03058-2
    1. Pike, Zebulon Montgomery, 1779-1813—Juvenile literature. 2. Explorers—West (U.S.)—Biography—Juvenile literature. 3. West (U.S.)—Description and travel—To 1848—Juvenile literature. 4. United States—Exploring expeditions—Juvenile literature. I. Title II. Series.
    [DNLM: 1. Pike, Zebulon Montgomery, 1779-1813. 2. Explorers.]
F592.P653S56    1990
917.704'2'092—dc20
[B]                                        90-2221
[92]                                        CIP
                                            AC

*Pikes Peak in the Colorado
Rocky Mountains*

# Table of Contents

# Chapter 1
# Pikes Peak

By November of that year, 1806, winter had already come to the Great Plains. There were patches of snow among the tall prairie grasses, and the buffalo and mustangs had left their grazing lands for shelter in the mountains. Lieutenant Zebulon Montgomery Pike and his fifteen companions felt the winter cold, too, as the wind whipped through their light cotton uniforms. They had thought their expedition would take them to a warm climate. They were, after all, on a mission authorized by President Thomas Jefferson to look for the source of the Arkansas River. This journey, they expected, would take them close to the Spanish territory of New Mexico.

*Winter scene of Colorado's Fern Lake, 80 miles (129 kilometers) from Denver*

But as the exploring party headed farther west, Pike realized he had made a terrible mistake. Winter in the eastern Colorado territory was even colder than the one he had experienced the year before. On that expedition, he had led his men nearly to Canada in search of the source of the Mississippi River. Now he found himself in charge of frozen, half-starved men riding horses that could barely stand. Pike was not sure if any of them would last even a few weeks longer. Maybe we will never see the "Mexican Mountains" we've heard so much about, he worried.

The ragged, dispirited group continued west. Fi-

*Snow-covered Pikes Peak*

nally, in the middle of the afternoon of November 15, Pike sat straight in his saddle and stared hard at the horizon to the northwest. He had seen something that looked, he said later, like "a small blue cloud." It disappeared, then reappeared. Was it a mountain peak rising out of the plains? Maybe I'm seeing things, thought the exhausted lieutenant. But when it appeared again, Pike could see it was not a cloud at all, but a magnificent peak rising above a rocky mountain chain. Pike's body shook as he got out his telescope and scanned the range. From north to south he could see no end to the beautiful rocky summits.

*Pikes Peak*

The others now saw the high peak and the mountain range, and they all shouted "three cheers for the mountains of Mexico!" Confident that the source of the Arkansas River was nearby and their mission nearly complete, Pike and his men continued toward the range.

But their hardships were not over. Each day was colder than the one before. The horses, with only bark and cottonwood leaves to eat, soon were too weak to carry their loads. One by one the horses fell and died. The men, too, were so exhausted they could barely go

*Buffalo grazing on the plains*

on. The high mountains looked farther away than ever. Finally Pike ordered his men to stop so they could hunt for buffalo meat and rest.

When their strength was restored, the group headed on. A few days later the men arrived at what is today Pueblo, Colorado. Pike decided this was a good site to build a fortified camp. The site, he believed, was about a day's journey from the base of the mountain. Once the camp was complete, an exploring party could set off and, once atop the "Grand Peak," as Pike called it, they could map the entire region.

On November 24, Lieutenant Pike and three others set off on foot for the high point of the mountain range. The peak loomed large, and the explorers expected it would take them no more than a few hours to reach it. Yet two days passed and the group was still far from their goal. The smaller Cheyenne Mountain still lay between them and the high mountain's base. Pike ordered the group to leave behind their provisions and to begin climbing Cheyenne Mountain. Darkness fell quickly, though, and the cold grew more and more bitter. Finally, the four were forced to seek shelter in a cave.

*View from a snow cave in Colorado's Rocky Mountains*

*A nineteenth-century engraving of the Rocky Mountains, showing Pikes Peak in the background*

The next day the sun greeted Pike and his men, and they remembered it was Thanksgiving Day—November 27, 1806. The day ahead, however, was to bring little happiness or comfort. When the party finally reached the top of the Cheyenne, they realized that the enormous summit beyond them was twice the climb they'd already made. In fact, it now appeared to be fifteen to sixteen miles (twenty-four to twenty-six kilometers) away. To make matters worse, a wide valley lay between the two mountains.

The four men stared across at the mountain they so desperately wanted to conquer. They stood in three feet (about a meter) of snow, and the temperature was four degrees below zero (minus twenty degrees Celsius). They had not eaten in two days. Half-frozen in his cotton uniform, Pike took in the magnificent scenery. The distant peak, he wrote, was "as high again as what we had ascended, and would have taken a whole day's march to have arrived at its base."

Despite the fact that the "Grand Peak" would forever after be associated with this young soldier, he was now as close to it as he would ever be. To continue the journey even to its base would mean certain death for all four. Lieutenant Pike gave his men orders to return to camp. After a few days' rest, the entire party would move on toward the mountains to the south.

As Pike climbed Cheyenne on that Thanksgiving Day, he may not have been moving step by step to the "Grand Peak." But now, looking back, it certainly can be said that he was climbing to the peak of his career. The remaining years of his brief life would bring some glory—and some controversy—but never another moment like this one. As Zebulon Pike looked out from Cheyenne to the much higher summit beyond him, he was literally looking at his own monument—the mountain that would soon be known by all as Pikes Peak.

Pike was not the first person to see the mountain; Indians and Spaniards had known about it long before. But the name Pikes Peak is the one that took hold. Thus the mountain stands as a kind of memorial to America's early explorers, many of whom were young soldiers like Zeb Pike.

These men were often ill-equipped for the extreme dangers they encountered on their expeditions. Many survived only through a combination of courage, strength, and good luck. They not only mapped the continent, but they also reported to a curious nation on the vast, beautiful Western wilderness. They also enlightened their fellow countrymen about the continent's native peoples. These expeditions—and the bravery and dedication of the explorers—would help make America a nation that one day would extend from sea to sea.

*Pikes Peak, as seen from the "Garden of the Gods," Colorado Springs*

## Chapter 2
## A Soldier's Son

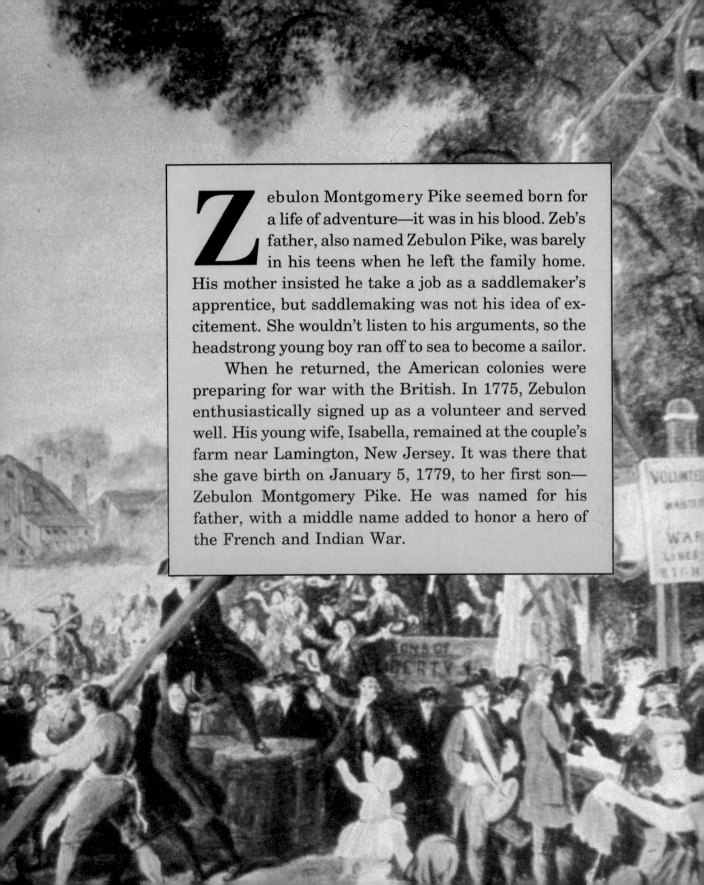

Zebulon Montgomery Pike seemed born for a life of adventure—it was in his blood. Zeb's father, also named Zebulon Pike, was barely in his teens when he left the family home. His mother insisted he take a job as a saddlemaker's apprentice, but saddlemaking was not his idea of excitement. She wouldn't listen to his arguments, so the headstrong young boy ran off to sea to become a sailor.

When he returned, the American colonies were preparing for war with the British. In 1775, Zebulon enthusiastically signed up as a volunteer and served well. His young wife, Isabella, remained at the couple's farm near Lamington, New Jersey. It was there that she gave birth on January 5, 1779, to her first son—Zebulon Montgomery Pike. He was named for his father, with a middle name added to honor a hero of the French and Indian War.

When the American Revolution was over in 1781, Zebulon Montgomery's father returned home and resumed farming. Before long he decided to move his family to a new farm in Bucks County, Pennsylvania, just across the Delaware River from New Jersey. He farmed there for several years before moving farther west to Northumberland County.

Like many farmers of his day, Zebulon Pike felt the urge to move even farther west. With the end of the American Revolution, the new United States looked even more toward westward expansion. Farmers from states along the East Coast were leaving to start new lives in Kentucky, Tennessee, and Ohio. Many of the Pike's friends and neighbors had left

*Settlers on the American frontier who made a clearing in the forest and built a crude log cabin*

*Marietta, Ohio, in 1788*

Pennsylvania for the Beautiful River, as they called it—the Ohio. They would journey first to Pittsburgh and then sail by flat-bottomed boat to one of the frontier towns such as Marietta or Cincinnati.

Captain Pike took his first trip west of Pittsburgh, however, not to look for new farmland but to serve once again as a soldier for his country. As American settlers poured into the territory known then as the Northwest, the native people living there made bold attempts to stop them. The Indians fought hard to protect their villages and hunting grounds from the white settlers. They knew their very survival was at stake.

Congress decided that the U.S. government would fight to protect its citizens from Indian attacks. In 1790, Congress gave President Washington the authority to call out volunteer militias in Kentucky, Virginia, and Pennsylvania to defend the American frontier. At first, however, these ragtag groups of men were woefully unprepared for the job. They were unruly, undisciplined, and terrified. They were as likely to run from battle as to stand and fight.

President Washington realized that his western Indian campaign would succeed only if he called up more troops and found experienced officers to lead them. Captain Zebulon Pike, now forty years old and the father of four, answered the call and joined the Pennsylvania militia. The new recruits—many of them recently let out of jails and poorhouses—and their leader were ordered to Pittsburgh and then put on barges for Cincinnati's Fort Washington.

The fighting encountered by the troops stationed at Fort Washington was brutal. In one attack along the Wabash River, near what is today Greenville, Ohio, the Indians surprised the militiamen just before sunrise. Unable to see the camouflaged Indians, the terrified soldiers were easy targets. Officers pleaded with their men to stay together and fight on, but most tried desperately to escape. The militia suffered a humiliating defeat.

In early spring of 1792, Congress called up regular forces of the U.S. Army to help in the effort to save American lives and property on the frontier. President Washington placed all the western troops under the command of General Anthony Wayne. General Wayne was a hero of several revolutionary war battles and a dedicated military man. His mission was to

*President George Washington*

*General Anthony Wayne training troops at Fort Washington, Ohio, in 1793*

make the western territories safe for American settlers. He set about accomplishing this mission with a zeal that earned him the nickname "Mad Anthony."

Captain Zebulon Pike joined General Wayne's command and prepared to move his entire family from their Pennsylvania farm to the rough settlement of Fort Washington. In late April 1793, the army began its move down the Ohio River to Cincinnati. Captain Pike, his wife, and their four children—including fourteen-year-old Zebulon Montgomery—said good-bye to their friends and neighbors and set sail for their new life in the western frontier.

*General James Wilkinson,
Army officer and adventurer*

As the barges approached Cincinnati, people lined the shore to greet the soldiers and their families. General Wayne was welcomed by Fort Washington's most recent commander, General James Wilkinson. Wilkinson was well known both as a brave soldier and as a wheeler-dealer. Some found him charming; others thought him pompous and self-serving. General Wayne disliked Wilkinson immediately and was glad he would soon be stationed elsewhere.

As for Captain Pike and his son Zebulon Montgomery, they became Wilkinson's friends. They idolized him as a war hero, a brave Indian fighter, and a gallant leader. The bond between the flamboyant Wilkinson and young Zeb Pike would last the rest of

*Fort Washington in Cincinnati, Ohio*

Pike's life. For better or worse, the explorer's entire career would be linked with that of the controversial general.

Life in a remote frontier outpost like Fort Washington was harsh and violent. Young Zebulon matured quickly in such a setting. He had attended a variety of "common schools," as they were called, and had been tutored by his father. But his education came to an end when he was fifteen. Like his father before him, he enlisted in the army. Zebulon had impressed many at Fort Washington with his energy, stubbornness, and bravery. These qualities would now be put to the test as young Private Pike put on a soldier's uniform and headed into the wilderness.

# Chapter 3
# On His Own

General Wayne wasted no time in whipping his 2,500 new recruits into shape. His mission was to make the western frontier safe for American settlers, and he had no time to waste on soldiers who didn't want to fight. Drills and training exercises were conducted for long hours each day. Minor offenses by anyone were punished by three dunkings in the frigid Ohio River. One hundred lashes on a bare back was the penalty for more serious misdeeds. In a matter of months, "Mad Anthony" had molded a strong fighting force.

Wayne's army, including the eager young Zebulon Pike, left Fort Washington early in 1794. From there they traveled north to Fort Recovery, near Greenville, the site of the earlier militia defeat. The troops rebuilt Fort Recovery, then moved farther north to build a new fort, Fort Defiance, in the heart of Indian country.

*General Wayne's defeat of the Indians at the Battle of Fallen Timbers*

When the Indians saw that the army was building a fort on their hunting grounds, they decided enough was enough and they prepared for battle. On August 20, 1794, the two forces clashed in the Battle of Fallen Timbers. The battle pitted a thousand American troops against five hundred Indians. After fighting for only forty-five minutes, the Indians withdrew. Only thirty-three Americans and nineteen Indians had been killed. But the American troops were better armed and supplied than ever before, and the Indians knew the two sides were no match.

The Indians tried to stay out of sight, hoping the Americans would move their forces elsewhere, but

*The signing of the Treaty of Greenville on August 3, 1795*

time was against them. They had been driven from their cornfields and hunting grounds, and their people were starving. What's more, the British in Canada had promised to send aid, but none had arrived. The chiefs knew their only choice was to either surrender or perish.

On August 3, 1795, the Indians signed the Treaty of Greenville, giving up all their lands in the Ohio country and eastern Indiana. American settlers along the Ohio could now live in peace, and westward migration began again. Settlers from the East quickly began arriving in Ohio and venturing even farther west from there.

*Fort Massac State Park in Metropolis, Indiana, where a replica of the old Fort Massac has been built*

Young Zebulon was soon sent farther west, too. General Wayne's orders directed Pike to "descend the Ohio with the same barge and crew with which you ascended and deliver the dispatches and stores committed to your charges to Captain Pike, commandant of Fort Massac." Fort Massac, located on the north bank of the Ohio, was in Illinois country, only forty miles (sixty-four kilometers) east of the Mississippi River. It was a vital link in the chain of forts that were being built on the frontier. According to the army's plans, the forts would eventually extend from Pittsburgh to the Gulf of Mexico.

Captain Pike, Zebulon's father, had just been put in charge of Fort Massac. His duties were to protect western pioneers and to inspect any river vessels moving from the Ohio to the Mississippi. There was a serious reason for inspecting the river traffic. Although the Treaty of Greenville had brought peace with the Indians, peace was still in danger. This time, however, the threat came not from the Indians but from the Spanish.

Spain possessed the coast of the Gulf of Mexico, the mouth of the Mississippi River, and the vast territory west of the Mississippi. The Spaniards were ever watchful of Americans' westward migration, which they saw as a threat to their North American holdings. They were willing to do whatever they could to discourage settlement on their vast western lands. If they had to, they would intimidate settlers and supply boats along the Mississippi and Ohio rivers.

*Heavy ship traffic at the mouth of the Mississippi River*

*Settlers traveling the Ohio River*

Many Americans, however, were determined to go as far west as they could. War with Spain was a risk they were willing, even eager, to take if it meant greater wealth and power. Private adventurers known as filibusterers organized expeditions from Ohio and Kentucky. These expeditions—not authorized by the U.S. government—were intended to unsettle relations between the United States and Spain.

The last thing the new American government needed, however, was a costly war with a major world power such as Spain. Captain Pike and his men, including his son Zebulon Montgomery, were to inspect the barges that passed down the Ohio toward the Mississippi. Any expeditions that seemed suspicious were to be halted.

Young Zebulon Pike spent most of the next five years inspecting supplies and then distributing them to the chain of forts along the Ohio and the Mississippi. These supplies were furnished by private merchants, who placed them on barges in Pittsburgh or Cincinnati. The barges then traveled down the Ohio, discharging their cargo along the way.

Zeb was often in charge of as many as twelve barges at a time. He learned quickly on his job, acquiring the leadership abilities of a much older man. Zeb's competency did not go unnoticed. On March 3, 1799, he was promoted to second lieutenant and, on November 1 of the same year, to first lieutenant.

*Settlers often traveled the Ohio River in flatboats, which could transport their livestock as well as their household belongings.*

Early in 1801, Lieutenant Pike was assigned to watch over the construction of a new fort just south of Fort Massac. The new fort was to be named Wilkinsonville after Pike's good friend General Wilkinson, then commander of the army. When the fort was completed, Pike became adjutant—that is, the assistant to the commanding officer. In the post of adjutant, Pike was on regular guard and police duty, and he also conducted battalion drills two or three times a week. There were company drills every day and officer drills once or twice a week.

But despite his heavy schedule, Pike still found time at night to improve his mind. He realized he would have to study hard to make up for his lack of formal education. He studied mathematics, French, and Spanish, and read whatever literature he could.

Life for the young officer, however, was not all work. On his trips up and down the Ohio River between 1795 and 1801, Pike made friends with many farmers and planters. He would stop at their homes to buy supplies and would often dine with their entire families. One family that he was particularly close to was that of Captain James Brown of Sugar Grove, Kentucky. In fact, the Brown family was related to Pike's mother.

As the months went by, Zebulon Montgomery fell in love with Clarissa Brown, the captain's eighteen-year-old daughter. When Pike was away, the two wrote long letters and soon began making plans to marry. Unfortunately, Clarissa's father was completely against the match. When Lieutenant Pike asked Captain Brown for his daughter's hand, the captain refused. But the couple decided to get married anyway, and they eloped to Cincinnati.

The two families were in an uproar. The elder Pikes traveled to Sugar Grove to hear Brown vent his anger. Captain Pike then wrote to his son for an explanation. Lieutenant Pike answered: ". . . and should I be confined to the walls of a prison, still shouldn't my soul be free. . . . Whilst I have the breath I will never be the slave of any man. . . ."

Clearly, the lieutenant had a mind of his own! Unfortunately, so did Captain Brown. There is no record that the son-in-law and his father-in-law ever saw each other after 1801. Likewise, there is no record that Captain Brown, a wealthy plantation owner, ever gave the young couple any money to supplement Pike's meager army salary.

*Pastoral scene in the Ohio River Valley*

Shortly after the marriage, Lieutenant Pike was assigned to a post on the banks of the Wabash River in eastern Indiana. Pioneers were quickly moving into this remote area north of the Ohio River, and a fort had been built to protect them. So, in the summer of 1802, Zebulon and Clarissa Pike moved to the newly built Fort Knox, which stood on the site of the old French settlement of Vincennes. It must have seemed like the very edge of civilization!

Vincennes was a depressing place. The heavy spring rains flooded the low banks of the Wabash, and the air was heavy and foul-smelling. The log cabins of the original French settlement were gradually being replaced by clapboard houses. Hunters in deerskin clothes and coonskin caps were still a common sight on the town's main street.

The Pikes lived inside Fort Knox, which was small and also built of logs. About one hundred troops with officers and their families were also housed within the fort's walls. There was little privacy, and squabbles among residents were frequent. Drinking, gambling, and fighting were also part of everyday life, much to Zeb Pike's dismay.

Early in 1803, the Pikes were transferred again, this time to Fort Kaskaskia, which lay along the Mississippi River about fifty miles (eighty kilometers) south of present-day St. Louis, Missouri. Kaskaskia had also been a French settlement in the early 1700s but had been taken by the British during the French and Indian War. It was, in turn, captured by the Americans during the revolutionary war. By 1803, there were about eighty families living there.

Another army officer also stationed at Fort Kaskaskia during this time was Meriwether Lewis. The

BRITISH AMERICA
CANADA
Claimed by the United States by discovery 1792 and Exploration 1805 - 1806
Columbia
TERRITORY OF LOUISIANA
Purchased from France in 1803
Missouri
Arkansas R.
Red R.
Territory claimed by United States as part of Louisiana Territory
SPANISH
MEXICO
Colorado
Rio Grande
Gulf of California
PACIFIC OCEAN
ATLANTIC OCEAN
GULF OF MEXICO
ILLINOIS TERRITORY
INDIANA TER.
MICHIGAN TERRITORY
OHIO
KENTUCKY
TENNESSEE
VIRGINIA
NORTH CAROLINA
SOUTH CAROLINA
GEORGIA
MISSISSIPPI TERRITORY
TERRITORY OF ORLEANS
SPANISH FLORIDA
PENNSYLVANIA
NEW YORK
NEW JERSEY
DELAWARE
VERMONT
MASS.
CONN.
L. WINIPEG
LAKE OF THE WOODS
L. NIPIGON
L. SUPERIOR
L. MICHIGAN
HURON
L. ONTARIO
LAKE ERIE
GREAT SALT L.
SAN FRANCISCO
SAN DIEGO
SANTA FE
ST. LOUIS
KASKASKIA
DETROIT
FT. DEARBORN
FT. WAYNE
COLUMBUS
CINCINNATI
FRANKFORT
NASHVILLE
CLEVELAND
PITTSBURG
PHILADELPHIA
WASHINGTON
RICHMOND
NORFOLK
CHESAPEAKE B.
RALEIGH
WILMINGTON
COLUMBIA
AUGUSTA
CHARLESTON
SAVANNAH
ST. AUGUSTINE
VICKSBURG
MOBILE
NEW ORLEANS
SEIZED BY U.S. 1810-1812
MONTREAL
QUEBEC
OSWEGO
BUFFALO
ALBANY
BOSTON
BAHAMA ISLANDS
MAP OF THE UNITED STATES 1810-1812
Longitude West from Greenwich

United States, under President Thomas Jefferson, had just purchased from France a vast chunk of land called Louisiana west of the Mississippi River. Jefferson commissioned Lieutenant Lewis, along with William Clark, to lead an expedition into the new territory. At Kaskaskia, Lewis was recruiting men for the trip. The exploring party would attempt to find a northwest route from St. Louis to the Pacific Ocean.

*The purchase of Louisiana from France added a vast new expanse of land to the American frontier.*

Lewis and Clark set off from St. Louis in May 1804. Shortly afterwards, Lieutenant Pike was asked by his old friend General Wilkinson if he, too, would lead an expedition into the Louisiana territory. Pike was to travel up the Mississippi River until he reached its source, commonly thought to be Leech Lake, in present-day Minnesota. Finally, Pike's years of hard work on the frontier would be put to good use.

# Chapter 4
# An Age of Exploration

In 1804, Zebulon Montgomery Pike turned twenty-five. He had been in the army nearly ten years, yet he'd seen little combat and had had few chances for real adventure or glory. He was still young and eager and, most of all, very ambitious. So when the call came from General Wilkinson to "proceed up the Mississippi with all possible diligence," Pike was happy to accept. An era of exploration had begun in America, and Zebulon Pike wanted to be a part of it.

At that time, the land west of the Mississippi was not well known. Maps had been made showing the general course of major rivers there, but their sources were not known and details were not clear. It was home to many Indian tribes, of course, and had been variously controlled by the French, British, and Spanish. Still, few United States citizens had ever set foot on it. The Spanish still held vast lands north of Mexico, and the British possessed what is today Canada. But suddenly—since the Louisiana Purchase of 1803—the French were almost entirely gone from the continent. Now the young American republic held a huge chunk of land in the middle of the continent, and Americans had to try to compete with European powers for valuable trading routes there.

*Much of the new land of the Louisiana Purchase was rich and fertile, like this Kansas prairie land.*

Many Europeans and Americans thought that the West had no value itself, that it was valuable only as a source of new trade routes to the Orient. The Europeans had been searching for a northwest passage to the Orient for nearly three hundred years. Many thought at first that, after crossing a single ridge of mountains in North America, they would be able to look out at the Pacific Ocean that reached to China. As they came to realize the vastness of the North American West, explorers hoped to find a west-flowing river that led to the Pacific.

When President Jefferson sent Lewis and Clark up the Missouri River to explore the Northwest in 1804, he wanted to know many things. How wide was the continent? What are its native people like? Is the land useful for anything? What Lewis and Clark found, of course, was not a wasteland but an enormous continent with an astonishing variety of animals, minerals, and other natural resources. All of a sudden, finding a route to the Orient was not as important as gaining easier access to the American interior and all of its natural riches. From this time on, the coonskin-capped explorer was not seen as just a curiosity but as an important player on the North American stage.

*Meriwether Lewis*

The exploration of the Western frontier attracted honest, loyal public servants, such as Zebulon Pike and Lewis and Clark. But it also attracted greedy scoundrels, interested only in personal gain. Some were willing to toss aside any loyalty to the United States if they could gain great wealth and power.

One such man was General James Wilkinson, whom Zebulon Pike first met at Fort Washington. Wilkinson was one of those looking for opportunities for his own gain. As the West began to open up to settlers and traders, Wilkinson saw that his best opportunity for financial gain lay in siding with Spain. The Spanish had become nervous about the number of pioneers heading westward. They knew that, sooner or later, it would be nearly impossible to keep American settlers out of their vast holdings in North America. Somehow, Spain had to prevent the settlement of their territory.

There were three possible ways to do this, and the Spanish tried all three. First, since Spain controlled the mouth of the Mississippi, they tried to stop western trade by denying Americans the "right of deposit" at New Orleans. Without an American port on the Gulf of Mexico, goods coming down the Mississippi would not be able to leave the country. This, however, did not interfere with the settlers. Next, the Spaniards sent agents into new American territories, such as Tennessee and Kentucky, to seize settlers' property. While this made life difficult for the settlers, it did not frighten them into staying near the East Coast. Third, they tried to separate the westernmost American territories and annex them to the Spanish empire. Spain knew that the United States probably did not yet have the military strength to

*General James Wilkinson*

fight for these faraway lands. So Spain's agents, one of whom was General Wilkinson, worked hard at acquiring them.

Wilkinson had made his first "business" trip to Spanish headquarters in New Orleans in 1787. He bribed his way into the company of the provincial governor and convinced him that settlers in Kentucky and Tennessee might welcome independence and affiliation with Spain. The governor paid Wilkinson handsomely for what the Spanish considered valuable information. They also allowed his barges, loaded with tobacco, flour, and whiskey, to pass down the Mississippi unharmed.

The profits from these shipments made Wilkinson very rich, and for a time, everyone was happy—Wilkinson because of his sudden wealth, and the Spanish because they believed Wilkinson's reports that Kentucky and Tennessee would soon be theirs. But Wilkinson spent his money so quickly that he soon needed another source of income. So he asked for a new position with the army. In 1791, he became Lieutenant Colonel Commandant; in a short time, he had command of the entire American army. Yet he was still a paid informant for the Spanish. Wilkinson, it seems, had become a skilled double agent.

Soon, however, Spain found it no longer needed Wilkinson's services. Kentucky, far from wanting to be allied with Spain, was admitted to the Union as the fifteenth state in 1792, and Tennessee became the sixteenth state in 1796. Finally, in 1800, Spain secretly ceded all of Louisiana to France. With French territory now lying between Spanish lands and the United States, Spain no longer had to worry about American settlement of its lands.

The new president, Thomas Jefferson, was happy to have the Spanish threat removed for the time being. He worried, though, about what kind of neighbors the French would be. He feared that any squabbling with them would lead to a permanent ban on American trade on the Mississippi River. In 1803 he sent James Monroe to Paris to discuss the situation with the Emperor Napoleon. To the utter amazement of the Americans, Napoleon offered the land for sale. In April 1803, the United States bought the entire territory of Louisiana for $15 million, more than doubling the country's size. To the equal surprise of the Spanish, they were once again neighbors with the Americans.

*Aaron Burr*

This new opportunity was not lost on General Wilkinson. When President Jefferson set about looking for a governor of Upper Louisiana—which included land north and west of St. Louis, all the way to Canada—Wilkinson made it known that he was keenly interested in the appointment. With all the military secrets that would be available to the governor, the Spanish would surely be willing to pay him even more for his valuable information.

Wilkinson threw himself into the contest for the governorship as zealously as if he were preparing for a battle. He knew he would need the help of an important politician if his appointment were to be confirmed by the president and Congress. Who better to have on his side than the president of the Senate, Aaron Burr?

*Alexander Hamilton (left) and Aaron Burr preparing for the duel in which Hamilton lost his life*

Burr was a powerful man in Washington, but he was not liked by many of President Jefferson's advisers. Jefferson felt that Burr had tried to steal the presidential election of 1800. Burr, for his part, felt the presidency had been taken away unfairly from him. He believed that the secretary of the treasury, Alexander Hamilton, was to blame. In any case, it was important that President Jefferson not find out about meetings between Burr and Wilkinson. If he knew about them, he would surely not support Wilkinson's appointment as governor.

Wilkinson, as usual, got what he wanted. In 1804 he became governor of Upper Louisiana, and he settled in St. Louis. Aaron Burr, however, was not so lucky. He met his political ruin in 1805, when he fought a duel with his old enemy, secretary of the treasury Alexander Hamilton.

Burr won the duel, but killed Hamilton in the process. The nation was outraged at Hamilton's death, and Burr left Washington in disgrace. Burr then looked toward the west, with its potential for development, to satisfy his longing for power.

With governors installed in both the upper and lower sections of Louisiana, Jefferson turned his attention to exploring the country's new territory. He wasted no time in sending an exploring party, led by Meriwether Lewis and William Clark, to the Pacific coast. The explorers headed up the Missouri River from St. Louis in May 1804.

In the meantime, Wilkinson, as governor of Upper Louisiana, also had the authority to send an exploring party into the region he governed. He told his old friend Lieutenant Zebulon Pike to head to St. Louis as quickly as possible and prepare to lead a party up the Mississippi River.

*Alexander Hamilton*

Wilkinson sent Pike on the Mississippi expedition without first telling President Jefferson. Given Wilkinson's reputation for shady dealings, many have wondered what his reasons were for such secrecy. It may have been nothing more than Wilkinson's desire to get the expedition underway quickly so the group could return before the harshest months of winter. Fortunately for Wilkinson, and for Pike, when Jefferson was finally told of the expedition, he gave it his blessing.

# Chapter 5
# Up the Mississippi

*July 30, 1805*

*Sir:*
*Having compleated your equipments you are to proceed up the Mississippi with all diligence. . . .*

*You will be pleased to take the course of the River . . . noting creeks, Highlands, Prairies, Islands, rapids, shoals, mines, quarries, Timber. . . .*

*It is interesting to government to be informed of the Population and residence of the several Indian nations, of the Quantity and Species of Skins and Furs they barter . . . and the People with whom they trade.*

*You will proceed to the main branch of the River, until you reach the source of it. . . .*

*Your obedient Servant,*
*James Wilkinson*

Pike's mission up the Mississippi had several objectives. As General Wilkinson's letter said, finding the source of the Mississippi River was only one—and not even the most important. Lieutenant Pike was also to collect information on the land and geography of the region, to study the northern Indian tribes, and to keep them at peace.

The general also wanted Pike to check into the fur trade in the Upper Mississippi region. Trading between Indians and French and British companies had been going on for more than a century, and some Europeans had become very wealthy from it. Now that this region belonged to the United States, the American government wanted to charge taxes on the goods sold on the Mississippi.

*A trading post of Great Britain's Hudson's Bay Company in the North American wilderness*

Unfortunately, Pike was poorly equipped for such an ambitious trip. First of all, he himself was an inexperienced explorer and, as he would soon learn, he badly needed the help of a second lieutenant. Also, the government was stingy with supplies. Pike's diary shows that he received the usual items: flour, whiskey, cornmeal, pork, gunpowder, salt, and tobacco, as well as lead, writing paper, ink, flags, hunting dogs, tents, clothing, and blankets. But the scientific equipment he took was very crude. Pike noted that, while he was able to get a watch, a thermometer, and an instrument to measure latitude, none of these instruments worked very well.

No army doctor was sent on the voyage, though several were available. And finally, despite the fact that one of the journey's goals was to try to make peace among Indian tribes, no interpreter was sent along. The explorers would have to find guides and interpreters along the way if they were to have any hope of communicating with the Indians.

Yet Pike didn't complain. He was full of confidence as he and his twenty men left Bellefontaine, a fort north of St. Louis, in their seventy-foot (twenty-one meter) keelboat. The lieutenant's first journal entry noted simply: "Sailed from my encampment, near St. Louis, at 4 o'clock P.M. on Friday the 9th of August 1805 . . . water very rapid. . . ."

Pike and his men enjoyed good sailing during the first part of the voyage. The Upper Mississippi was very wide in places and dotted with many small islands. The surrounding countryside was made up of flower-filled prairie and dense forests. The numerous channels among these islands caused the explorers to lose speed from time to time.

As summer turned to fall, however, the journey became more difficult. Heavy rains damaged supplies and soured the men's spirits. Delays caused by navigating the channels became longer and more irritating. What's more, the boat was often damaged by stumps, logs, and sandbars.

Then, near what is today Keokuk, Iowa, the party met a new obstacle—rapids. These were eleven miles (eighteen kilometers) long and extended from shore to shore. "We found great difficulty," Pike noted with his usual understatement. In fact, he doubted if they would make it through at all. To get past rapids in those days, travelers had to attach ropes to their boats and trudge along the shore towing them. Even for a short distance, this was an arduous task.

*Wilderness trappers drying out their moccasins over a campfire as they make camp at night*

*Indian agent William Ewing*

They had just passed the first and most difficult shoal when they were met by several Indian canoes. Some of Pike's men reached for their rifles as the boats came closer. The lieutenant stared hard at the approaching Indians. His look changed from worry to relief, though, as he saw that one boat carried not only an American flag but a government official as well. They've come to help, Pike exclaimed, and he ordered his men to put down their guns.

In one canoe was an Indian agent named William Ewing, appointed by the government to teach farming techniques to the Sac Indians. With him were a French interpreter, four Sac chiefs, and fifteen Sac warriors. They quickly began transferring some of the heavy supply barrels to the Indian canoes. Now traveling much lighter, the expedition continued up the rapids without any trouble.

Just above the rapids lay Ewing's headquarters and a Sac village. The expedition stayed there several days and Pike made his first speech to an assembly of local chiefs. The speech was repeated many times during the expedition. As Pike wrote in his journal, he told them "that their great father, the president of the United States, wishing to be more intimately acquainted with the situation, wants, &c. of the different nations of the red people, in our newly acquired territory of Louisiana, had ordered the general [Wilkinson] to send a number of his young warriors . . . to take them by the hand, and make such enquiries. . . . I then presented them with some tobacco, knives, and whiskey."

Not all the Indians the group encountered were so friendly. Some were armed and looked quite menacing as they canoed alongside Pike's boat. But since Pike's men were armed, too, the Indians kept a safe distance. The Indians believed the Americans to be just as dangerous as Pike's group thought the Indians might be. Pike encouraged the Indians in this notion by trying to look very angry and menacing as his men sailed their boats past an Indian camp.

Still, one of Pike's missions was to convince the Indians that the Americans were their friends. The Indians thought very highly of the European traders, and the Americans realized the tribal chiefs would quickly side with the Europeans in any conflict. As Pike's journal notes: "It is astonishing to me, what a dread the Indians have of the Americans in this quarter. . . . It appears evident to me that the traders have taken great pains to impress on the minds of them an idea of our being a very vindictive, ferocious and Warlike People. . . ."

*Bluffs near Prairie du Chien on the upper Mississippi River*

It was early September by the time the expedition arrived at the old French settlement of Prairie du Chien, French for "dog's meadow." The town, in present-day southwestern Wisconsin, lay on small, beautiful prairie a mile (1.6 kilometers) from the Mississippi and four miles (six kilometers) north of the mouth of the Wisconsin River. Prairie du Chien was by far the largest town they had seen on the journey. Pike estimated there were between five hundred and six hundred white settlers. The town was once a trading center for Indians in the area, and later became a major French fur-trading post. Many wealthy traders of Prairie du Chien had built lovely homes there.

*A Winnebago camp*

Pike thought Prairie du Chien would make an excellent site for a military post, so he stayed for several days to explore the area. The Indians invited Pike's men to join them in an athletic contest, pitting their young warriors against Pike's soldiers. Pike wrote proudly in his journal, "My men beat all the villagers jumping and hopping."

At Prairie du Chien, Pike stocked up on supplies and acquired additional boats, including barges and canoes, to help carry them. Two men from the settlement also agreed to travel with Pike as interpreters.

*An Indian ceremony in which they face west to honor the setting sun*

Two days north of Prairie du Chien, the men visited a Sioux village. Pike had gotten used to the friendliness of the tribes he'd encountered so far. So he was completely surprised to be greeted by a hail of gunfire as he and his men came ashore. They ran back to their boats as the puzzled Indians watched. Finally, Pike realized the shots had been fired as a kind of welcome. He and his men then returned, somewhat nervously, to shore. This time they were greeted by the chief, who invited Pike into his lodge. There the two men sat on mats and smoked a peace pipe.

The expedition did not stay long at the village, despite the warm huts and hearty food the Sioux provided. Winter was coming and the strong north wind would soon make sailing very difficult. For now, though, the weather was pleasant enough that Pike could still marvel at the beauty of the landscape.

The party stopped at present-day Winona, Minnesota, and several men, including Pike, went hunting. Pike wrote: "On the right we saw the mountains . . . and the Prairie in their rear; and like distant clouds, the Mountains at the Prairie Le Cross; on our left and under our feet, the Valley between the two Barren Hills, through which the Mississippi wound itself by numerous channels, forming many beautiful

*Boatmen navigating a keelboat on the upper Mississippi River, as Indians follow in a canoe*

islands, as far as the eye could embrace the scene. Our four Boats under full Sail, their flags streaming before the wind, was altogether a prospect so variegated and romantic, that a man may scarcely expect to enjoy such a one above twice or thrice in the course of his life."

Unfortunately, shortly after they reached Lake Pepin—not really a lake at all but a very wide place in the Mississippi—they ran into trouble. They tried to cross the lake at night to avoid the daytime winds. "At first the breeze was very gentle," Pike wrote, "and we sailed with our Violins and other Music playing; but the sky afterwards became cloudy and quite a gale arose." The boats were finally forced to land.

*Engraving of a view on the upper Mississippi River*

On shore the men found another stranded voyager, a friendly Scotsman named Murdock Cameron. Cameron didn't seem bothered by his predicament and entertained Pike's voyagers with stories he'd heard during his travels in the region. He pointed to a faraway cliff called Maiden's Rock and told of an Indian girl who had climbed the hill singing her own death song. It seems she had been forced to give up the man she loved and instead was to marry someone she hated. Rather than submit to her people's wishes, she left her camp and headed up the cliff. Before anyone could stop her, she leaped from the highest point to her death.

When the storm weakened, Pike's men continued up the winding river. Only a little farther lay the mouth of the St. Peter's River, now called the Minnesota River, and the Falls of St. Anthony, at present-day Minneapolis. This stretch of the Mississippi River was one long, narrow rapid. Pike looked around him and saw high hills covered with maple, ash, and cedar trees. Wild geese and ducks were all around. The wilderness, Pike wrote, though often frightening, was a place of great beauty.

Pike stayed in this area for several days, exploring the land on both sides of the river's banks. He finally decided to ask the Sioux for a piece of land at the juncture of the St. Peter's and the Mississippi, on which to build a military camp. On September 23 he held a council with the Sioux chiefs and warriors. Lieutenant Pike signed a treaty purchasing 100,000 acres (40,469 hectares) lying on either side of the river. Pike received the land he needed for a military fort (later named Fort Snelling) and the Indians received gifts worth two hundred dollars.

*The Falls of St. Anthony on the Mississippi River at present-day Minneapolis, Minnesota*

Pike was extremely happy with both the site and the terms of its purchase. When General Wilkinson heard about the deal, however, he seems to have been less enthusiastic, remarking that Pike was a "much better soldier than negotiator."

The expedition still had far to go to reach the Mississippi's source. Before leaving the Falls of St. Anthony, Pike wrote what he called "a last adieu to the civilized world" and sent copies to his wife and General Wilkinson. He knew the next weeks and months would put his strength to the most difficult test.

# Chapter 6
# The Source

eaving the Falls of St. Anthony, the explorers found the current so swift that the boats had to be carried overland for quite a distance. Above the falls, the river became deep and narrow. The land was flatter, the countryside peaceful. By early October the nighttime temperatures were already reaching zero degrees Fahrenheit (minus eighteen degrees Celsius). Snow had begun to fall. Fortunately, the woods and prairie along the river were full of elk, bear, deer, beaver, buffalo, raccoons, and fowl. Usually two men would spend most of each day hunting. They would comb the shoreline areas for meat and game, all the while keeping up with the canoes on the river. Sometimes Lieutenant Pike, himself an excellent marksman, would walk with the hunters.

As the expedition traveled farther north into the cold Minnesota wilderness, each day became an exact copy of the one before. The group would rise early, break camp around six, and travel the river for two hours before stopping for breakfast. The day's main meal would then be at one o'clock in the afternoon. The men's favorite dish was meat, usually boiled in a pot with flour, wild rice, or corn.

After dinner, the expedition would continue up-river until dark, when they would stop to set up camp. After the evening meal the men would sit around their huge fire, talking, playing cards, or playing fiddles. They would wrap themselves in blankets to stay warm and sleep as close to the fire as they dared. Two men were always on guard duty, changing every two hours. At each change, new logs were added to the fire.

Lieutenant Pike nearly always slept in one of the tents set up to protect the supplies from the rain or snow. Every night he would update his charts and notes and write in his journal. It was often so cold that his ink would freeze in the bottle.

By the end of October, the snow and cold were making travel very difficult. Pike now realized that he would not be able to reach the river's source before the end of the year. He had hoped at least to reach Crow Wing River, near present-day Brainerd, Minnesota, before setting up winter camp. Crow Wing River was the northernmost point ever reached by traders canoeing up the Mississippi River. But even this goal proved too much for the expedition. The men were becoming weak and sick from the rigors of the journey. Pike knew he must stop, if only to save his crew, who were "killing themselves to obey my orders."

*Winter snows in the Minnesota wilderness made traveling and hunting difficult.*

Pike finally chose a site for the group's winter camp. According to his journal, they had now traveled over 233 miles (375 kilometers) north of the Falls of St. Anthony. The spot seemed ideal—there was plenty of meat and game, and the woods were thick with fine trees. The men began at once to build a stockade. The plan was for about half of the group to remain at the stockade while Pike led the rest toward Leech Lake, which he believed to be the river's source.

By November 1, the new canoes were ready and the small exploring party set to continue north. At launching, though, one canoe sank, and the crew now had to wait for another to be built. Finally, on December 10, after weeks of frustration and boredom, Lieutenant Pike and eleven soldiers left the stockade for the last leg of their journey.

Bringing in the Caribou

*Hunters hauling their game through the snow on a sled*

The river was by now partly frozen and the group needed two sleds to haul supplies. Each sled was dragged by two soldiers, and six others pulled the canoes. Along the river north of the stockade lay miles of snow-covered prairies. The group struggled to cover five miles (eight kilometers) a day. Four days into the trek, a sled broke through the ice, badly damaging its contents of Pike's own baggage, books, and cartridges. Once again, the expedition stopped for repairs. Once again, the delay caused extreme boredom, which Pike referred to as "fantastic of the brain."

Each new day brought stronger, colder winds and more dangerous travel. Pike walked ahead of the sleds, exploring, building fires to warm the men, choosing camp sites. "Never did I undergo more fatigue," he wrote in his journal, "in performing the duties of hunter, spy, guide, commanding officer. . . . At night I was scarcely able to make my notes intelligible."

By late December the river was completely frozen and the canoes were loaded onto the sleds. Three, sometimes four men dragged each sled. By Christmas Day the men reached the mouth of Crow Wing River, the spot where Pike had hoped to build his winter camp several months earlier.

On January 2, 1806, a guard yelled to the weary soldiers sitting around their fire that a party of Indians was headed their way at full speed. The men quickly armed themselves. They had never before met up with the Chippewa (also called the Ojibwa), but they believed them to be an especially warlike tribe. The approaching party, for their part, did not know what to expect either. They had noticed the campfire and had expected to meet their bitter enemies, the Sioux. Neither Pike's soldiers nor the Chippewa could have hoped for such a friendly meeting.

In the company of the Chippewa were an Englishman and a Frenchman, both employees of England's Northwest Fur Company. The Englishman, Cuthbert Grant, invited Pike to come with him to his headquarters on Cedar Lake, a few miles northeast of what today is Brainerd, Minnesota. When they arrived, Pike found a British flag flying over the settlement. He was indignant to find that British fur traders had a post in this area. But Grant quickly assured him that the flag simply belonged to the Indians.

*Drawing of a Sioux chief, from a painting by George Catlin*

*Sandy Lake, Minnesota*

The group then continued north on the narrowing river. Pike's mission almost ended disastrously when, on the night of January 4, several of his tents caught fire. Pike lost not only the tents but his bedding, leggings, moccasins, and socks. On January 8, the group took refuge at another of Cuthbert Grant's trading posts, this one near Sandy Lake. Here Pike enjoyed a short period of warm, dry rest and relaxation.

At the Sandy Lake trading post, the party planned the journey to Leech Lake—the last lap of the journey. They knew it would be an extremely difficult and dangerous trek, so they built lighter sleds, each one built from a large plank. They left on January 20, but soon discovered they had overloaded the sleds and so had to repack their supplies. Finally, by January 22, Pike and his men were on their way.

A settlement of log cabins and Indian homes in the early nineteenth century, built at the mouth of Minnesota's St. Croix River

Pike and his Indian guide again blazed the trail ahead of the sleds. They followed the narrow Mississippi as it twisted its way toward the northwest. A few days later they reached a fork in the river. One part continued northwest toward Lake Winnibigoshish, Lake Cass, and finally Lake Itasca, the true source of the river. The other fork would take the explorers west through a wide meadow and, they believed, to the river's source at Leech Lake. The men headed in this direction.

Northern Minnesota is dotted with hundreds of lakes. Any trails that might have guided the soldiers were covered with ice and snow. By now, the "Father of Waters" was a tiny stream and very hard to follow. The frozen, rocky ground made walking very difficult. The cold was nearly unbearable.

Finally, on the afternoon of February 1, Lieutenant Pike spotted Leech Lake. "I will not attempt to describe my feeling on the accomplishment of my voyage," Pike wrote in his journal after arriving on the shores of Leech Lake on February 1, "for this is the main source of the Mississippi."

Pike knew that British traders had a Northwest Fur Company trading post in the area and so set off to find it. Once there, he was well taken care of and able to rest for several days while he waited for the rest of his expedition to arrive. Several days later he met with some chiefs and warriors of the Chippewa

*Members of rival trading companies trying to win the goodwill of a group of Indians*

tribe. He explained why he had come and told how the Great Father in Washington wished for the Chippewa to make peace with their old enemy, the Sioux. He invited the chiefs to accompany him back to St. Louis for a council with General Wilkinson.

The lieutenant was very disappointed when all the Indians refused his offer. Wilkinson, Pike knew, wanted him to return with at least one Chippewa chief. Pike tried desperately to convince them to come along, finally telling the warriors that their enemy the Sioux would think them very cowardly if they did not come. Finally, two young warriors agreed to go.

*A Sioux encampment on the upper Mississippi River*

Feeling certain that his expedition would be considered a success, Pike now felt ready to begin his return trip. On March 1, the group headed for home. Their first major destination was the stockade where Pike had left half his men for the winter.

The reunion, at first, was a happy one, but any joy was soon clouded by reports of his men's conduct while he was gone. They had eaten all the meat stored for the return voyage and had either drunk all the whiskey or sold it to the Indians. Pike's own trunk of personal belongings had been vandalized. Pike demoted the men who were responsible for the destruction. He threatened harsher punishment, perhaps death, should there be any more trouble.

The Mississippi was still frozen in early March, and Pike's party had to wait several more weeks before they could begin their journey downriver. Pike passed the time exploring the region around Spunk River (between present-day Little Falls and St. Cloud, Minnesota) and getting to know the Menominee Indians who lived in the area.

The river was open to travel the first week of April. The night before their departure, the final preparations were complete. "In the evening," Pike noted in his journal, "the men danced to the violin and sang songs until eleven o'clock, so rejoiced was every heart at leaving this savage wilderness."

The trip downriver was as uneventful as the one upriver had been thrilling. The expedition needed less than three weeks to travel all the way back to St. Louis. On April 30, 1806, Pike and his men arrived in St. Louis, ending a trip that had taken nine months and covered more than 5,000 miles (8,047 kilometers).

Did Lieutenant Pike and his men accomplish all

*St. Louis, a fortified settlement along the Mississippi River*

they had set out to do? General Wilkinson seems to have thought so, for he soon had a new assignment for the weary soldier.

History's view of the first American expedition up the Mississippi, however, is mixed. Pike did not reach the true source of the river, but that fact is less important than some other failures. He had failed to stop illegal fur trading by Europeans, and he had failed to make peace among the Indian tribes. The two Indians whom Pike had persuaded to return to St. Louis with him ran away shortly after leaving their tribe. How could General Wilkinson hold a tribal peace council when not a single Indian warrior would attend?

*Sunset on the Mississippi River*

As for the new scientific and geographic information Pike was to gather, he did not find a single lake or stream that had not been previously discovered or named. What's more, his maps were poorly drawn and full of errors, and his journal betrays the bad conditions under which it was written.

Still, the publication of the journal in 1810 sparked new interest in the Upper Mississippi Valley. Pike's

*Fort Snelling, built upon land that Pike purchased from the Indians*

journey helped establish the present border between the United States and Canada as it extends from the Great Lakes to the Rockies. Also, valuable pieces of land were acquired for military use, such as the land that became Fort Snelling, a very important western post. And, perhaps most significantly, Pike acquired the experience and skills he would need for the more difficult expedition to follow.

*Chapter 7*
*The Journey West*

When Lieutenant Zeb Pike returned to St. Louis in the spring of 1806, he expected, if not a hero's welcome, at least a quick promotion and a few weeks' rest. Unfortunately, he was not given either. A promotion to captain was not even discussed for several months. And, instead of a vacation, Pike was immediately put to work by General Wilkinson preparing for another expedition—this one to the Western territories to look for the sources of the Arkansas and Red rivers.

The prospect of another long separation must have hit Lieutenant Pike's wife, Clarissa, hard. All alone, she had coped with the birth and death of a baby and had nursed her three-year-old daughter, Clara, back to health after a severe illness. Clarissa herself was often in poor health, too. Surely she must have looked forward to a long home visit from her husband, from whom she had heard very little for months.

Still, Clarissa Pike knew her husband well. He was a dutiful, ambitious soldier with a stubborn loyalty to his commander, General Wilkinson. If Wilkinson ordered Pike to the ends of the earth—as it must have seemed he was doing—Clarissa knew her husband would go.

General Wilkinson's letter outlined the objectives of the western expedition. The first one was to return Osage Indian prisoners that had been taken captive by the Potawatomie several months earlier. Pike was to take them back to their home at the Grand Osage Village, near the present-day Kansas-Missouri border. Wilkinson wrote that this was "the primary object of your expedition, and therefore you are to move with such caution, as may prevent surprise from any hostile band. . . ."

That done, Pike was then to turn his attention to the "accomplishment of a permanent peace between the Kanses [Kansas] and Osage nations," and arrange a meeting between the head chiefs of those nations. He was also to try to "establish a good understanding" with the Comanches. The general warned later in his letter that these missions might lead him close to the sources of the Arkansas and Red rivers—in other words, near the Spanish province of New Mexico. "There it will be necessary . . . ," Wilkinson wrote vaguely, "to prevent alarm."

As soon as Pike received the general's orders, he set to work preparing for the journey. He asked eighteen men from the Mississippi expedition to accompany him on this one as well. This time he would also take a doctor, an interpreter, and two privates. General Wilkinson's son, Lieutenant James B. Wilkinson, would also go along. The group would start with two

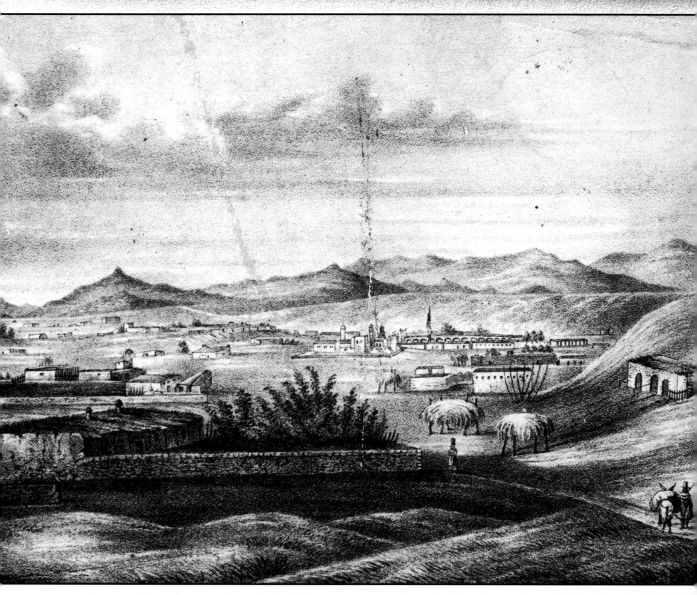

large river boats, instead of just one, as they had on the Mississippi. In fact, in almost every way, this mission was better equipped than the earlier one. Unfortunately, though, Pike decided that since the weather would be much warmer in the West—so near to Mexico, as he thought—he would not need to take heavy winter clothing. Cotton rather than wool uniforms would be enough, he thought. This misjudgment was almost fatal to the entire mission.

*Santa Fe, the Spanish capital of the New Mexico province*

Three weeks after receiving the general's orders, Pike's expedition was ready to leave. Pike had moved his family to Fort Bellefontaine, north of St. Louis near the juncture of the Mississippi and Missouri rivers. There they remained until his return. From this fort, on July 15, 1806, the expedition of twenty-three Americans and fifty-one Osage men, women, and children headed west up the broad Missouri River.

Navigating the Missouri River proved to be much harder than Pike had expected. Each boat was equipped with a square sail and mast, but the current was too treacherous for sailing and so these soon were taken down. Instead, the soldiers either rowed or, when the river was too shallow, pushed the boats by

*Herds of bison and elk along the upper Missouri River*

leaning on long poles stuck deep in the riverbed. In this way the boats could cover about ten to fifteen miles (sixteen to twenty-four kilometers) a day.

Nearly constant rain also slowed the explorers. Many men became sick and were unable to do their share of the work. Still, the land between St. Louis and the Grand Osage Village was so full of deer, buffalo, turkeys, and geese that all members of the party were able to eat to their fill. When the sun finally did appear, Pike noted that this land was "one of the most beautiful the eye ever beheld."

*Long poles were sometimes used to push boats down a river when the current was slow or the water was shallow.*

*A landscape scene in the mountains of the far West*

The party arrived at the Grand Osage Village in mid-August. The village was made up of several lodges, housing nearly a thousand Indians, formed in a large circle. The Osage were overjoyed to have their people returned, and they showed their gratitude by treating the soldiers extremely well—at first, anyway.

About a week after arriving in the village, Pike held a council with representatives from both the great and little Osage tribes. The Little Osage, a much smaller tribe, lived about six miles (ten kilometers) away. Pike gave a speech that was similar to the one he had given to the Indians of the Upper Mississippi. He explained that the Indians' land now lay within the United States and that the Father in Washington wanted peace among all tribes. Then he passed out medals and gifts.

This time, Pike asked to buy horses for the overland journey to the villages of the Pawnee and Kansas Indians. Much to Pike's surprise, the Osage refused. The captain raised the price several times until, finally, they agreed to sell him fifteen horses. The chief also agreed to send along thirty warriors to help the expedition. Pike then exchanged his boats for supplies. He was now ready to continue his journey overland, and on August 26 he headed into Kansas.

Unfortunately, no sooner had Pike's men left than the Osage began telling traders and Indian agents that Pike had stolen their horses. What's more, the Indians claimed that Pike had not returned all their prisoners. Pike, for his part, found the Indians' horses too weak for the journey. Many dropped from exhaustion only a few days out of the Osage village. It seems that Pike's visit had done more harm than good for relations between the Osage and the Americans.

*Land that was once the home of North America's Plains Indians*

*Modern-day view of the Great Plains, which Zebulon Pike called the Great American Desert*

Zebulon Pike and his men were the first Americans to make an expedition into the Kansas plains. As he left the Osage River, just over the Missouri-Kansas line, as far as he could see lay "prairie rising and falling in regular falls." He went on to refer to the Great Plains as the "Great American Desert" and compared the land to the deserts of Africa, where "not a speck of vegetable matter existed." For many years, people believed that this great "prairie ocean" formed a barrier that settlers would never cross.

*A Pawnee attacked by grizzly bears during a hunting trip*

As Pike's group headed northwest into Pawnee Indian country, they received word from Pawnee hunters that hundreds of Spanish soldiers had recently passed nearby. Pike wrote in his journal that he did not know why the Spanish troops were in the area, but he surely must have guessed the reason—they were looking for him. General Wilkinson had warned Pike that if the Spanish got wind of his mission they would surely try to stop him. The Spanish thought Lieutenant Pike might be a common spy.

Pike heard more about the Spanish troops when he and his men arrived at the Pawnee village in Nebraska Territory in late September. The Pawnee chief told him that six hundred Spanish soldiers had recently spent more than a week at the village. What a sight they had been, riding across the plains! Their leader, Lieutenant Malgares, and two other officers led on jet-black stallions, while all the others rode white horses. The Spaniards were very friendly to the Pawnee and gave all the warriors shiny gold medals and Spanish flags. They asked only one thing—that when Pike and his men arrived, the Pawnee must stop them from going farther.

Captain Pike was not disturbed by this news. He met with the Indians, gave his speech, and asked them to give up their Spanish medals and flags. The Indians refused. Pike at first insisted but soon realized that, if he continued, the Indians would become angry enough to actually stop his expedition from heading farther west.

Pike, too, spent many days among the Pawnee. He seems to have found the Plains Indians—including also the Comanche and the Apache—extremely interesting. He observed them carefully and wrote about them in great detail.

The Indians, however, were too impressed by their recent Spanish visitors to pay much attention to Pike and his men. If these shabby-looking men are representatives of the Great American Father, the Indians thought, we will side with Spain any day. After more than a week at the village, Pike was ordered to leave by the Pawnee chief. You must leave quickly, he told Pike, or the Pawnee will be forced to make good on their promise to the Spanish.

Pike left the Pawnee village "considerably per-turbed." He had gotten a few more horses, but again at a high price. He left knowing that the tribe would side with Spain in any conflict. He had also failed to bring peace between the Pawnee and Kansas tribes.

In early October they continued their journey, heading southwest back through Kansas. After sev-eral days they arrived at the Arkansas River and set up camp near what is today Larned, Kansas. This was the spot where the group would now split. Lieutenant Wilkinson was to lead one group down the Arkansas till it met the Mississippi. Pike would head upriver until he reached its source. They stayed at camp several days making buffalo-skin canoes for the men who would journey downriver.

*Pike's men hunted buffalo on the Great Plains for food and hides.*

On October 28, Lieutenant Wilkinson, four privates, and a few remaining Osage warriors left in two canoes. Expecting to reach the Mississippi in twenty-two days, they took enough food to last a month. Instead, the journey took seventy-three days. As they headed down the Arkansas they became the first American expedition into what is now Oklahoma.

The next day Pike and his men, including John Robinson, the expedition doctor, headed west along the Arkansas on horseback. As they moved farther and farther west, they saw the buffalo, deer, and elk moving toward the mountains. By mid-November the cold north winds were whipping across the plains. Pike worried that the winter would be more severe than he had predicted—maybe even worse than last year's near the source of the Mississippi.

*Elk grazing on the snowy plains*

*Clouds at the top of Pikes Peak*

The group was overjoyed on November 15 when they spotted the peak that "appeared like a small blue cloud" hovering over a distant mountain chain. They thought these majestic "Mexican Mountains" formed the boundary between the provinces of Louisiana and New Mexico.

On November 24, believing they were close to the Arkansas River's source, Pike had his men build a stockade alongside the river where Pueblo, Colorado, stands today. From there he and three others embarked on what he thought would be a one-day march to the summit of the "blue mountain." But the dangerous three-day climb up Cheyenne Mountain convinced the captain that to go on would undoubtedly kill them all. Pikes Peak, the "Grand Peak . . . on which rests eternal snows," would have to be left behind. "I believe no human being could have ascended to its pinical," Pike wrote. With a heavy heart, he ordered his men back to the stockade at Pueblo.

# Chapter 8
## "Is This Not the Red River?"

When Pike and his three companions got back to the stockade, there was more bad news. A fierce snowstorm had pounded the tiny building. The men had not been able to hunt, and now the food supply was nearly gone. There was no grass for the horses and they, too, were near starvation. And the storm continued to rage.

Captain Pike decided to wait out the storm and then push on. He was determined to find the Arkansas's source, as well as the Red River's. Three days of hard travel brought the group to the Royal Gorge near present-day Canon City, Colorado. There Pike tried to find the trail recently followed by the Spanish soldiers on their way back to Santa Fe.

*Moonrise over the Rockies*

After a few days the men found a worn trail—worn down by the hooves of the Spaniards' horses, Pike thought. The trail headed north, but Pike believed it would soon veer south again and lead him to the headwaters of the Red River. He soon learned, however, that he was not following the Spanish trail at all. Instead it was an old Indian trail, which ended at an abandoned camp.

He was bitterly disappointed. He and his men had followed the trail a considerable distance north—they were now among some of the highest peaks of what we know today as the Colorado Rockies. But they were no nearer the Red River.

The men then headed south, soon finding another stream, which they correctly identified as the South Platte River. After following it southward for a few days, they left the South Platte and followed another stream—this one must be the Red River, they thought. Pike ordered some of his men to continue south along the river. He and two others, however, headed upriver to see how far away its source might be and if there were a chance of reaching it.

After several days of difficult travel on foot along the twisting, narrow river, the group reached a high point. From there Pike scanned the countryside. The river continued for at least thirty miles (forty-eight kilometers) more—beyond that Pike couldn't tell. But following it to its source would be dangerous, if not deadly, for a fierce snowstorm was raging.

*View on the South Platte River*

*Winter travel in the Western mountain regions was both exhausting and dangerous.*

It was Christmas Eve when the expedition was reunited near present-day Salida, Colorado. Pike was distressed to hear of his men's sufferings. No one had the proper clothing for below-zero temperatures, and they had long since turned their bedding into socks and makeshift cloaks. The men were now sleeping on the bare ground without blankets. The only way they survived the frigid nights was to build huge fires and lie as close to them as they dared—"One side burned while the other was pierced by cold winds."

On Christmas Day, Pike decided to give up his search for the Spanish trail and instead head back to the plains. They would follow the stream on which

*A blustery day in the mountains*

they were now camped, the stream Pike believed to be the Red River. The horses were now either dead or useless, so the men built sleds for the supplies.

A few days downriver, on January 5, 1807, Pike realized that this stream came through the same pass he had first seen a month earlier. Clearly this was not the Red River—it was instead the Arkansas! "This was a great mortification," Pike wrote in his journal. He still had not located the Red River. Ice and snow continued to hamper their journey, and the men were half-frozen and half-starved. "This was my birth-day," Pike wrote that day, "and most fervently did I hope never to pass another so miserably."

*Sunset in the Sangre de Cristo Mountains of New Mexico*

The group now headed downriver to their old campsite at Royal Gorge. Here they decided to build another stockade, replenish the food supply for those unable to travel, and then those who could would continue south. When they had crossed the Sangre de Cristo Mountains, which lay almost on the border of New Mexico, scouts would then return to the stockade to retrieve the disabled men.

One of Pike's soldiers called the next few days' march "more than human nature could bear . . . three days without sustenance through snow three feet deep, with burdens only fit for horses." Fortunately, one of the men killed a buffalo, which was all that prevented the explorers from starving. The cold never let up, though, and soon ten out of the twenty still left in the party had feet too frozen to walk.

On January 27 the explorers arrived at a small stream, which they again hoped might be the Red River. They followed it south as it passed through high mountain ranges. The valley became a winding desert of sand dunes. Atop one of the dunes, Pike took out his telescope and caught sight of a large river running west. It was about fifteen miles (twenty-four kilometers) away.

They reached the large river's bank on January 30. They continued south a few miles before finally stopping at a wooded area, where they built a stockade. Pike was relieved to have reached a point of safety—a secure fort away from the extreme cold to the north. What he didn't know was that he had been following the Rio Grande River, not the Red, and that he had built his fort well into Spanish territory.

When the stockade was built, Pike sent five men back to find those left in the mountains. On February 9, Dr. Robinson left the expedition and headed for Santa Fe, in the Spanish province of New Mexico. It seems he had a business matter to clear up with someone there. The real reasons for Dr. Robinson's journey are not clear—surely he and Pike must have known that he would be stopped by the Spaniards and questioned. Did he want to draw attention to Pike's expedition, now camped west of the Rio Grande?

*Old Santa Fe*

Pike stayed at the fort to work on his papers, maps, and journals. His period of rest and quiet did not last long, however, because on February 16, two Spanish soldiers rode up to the stockade for a talk with the captain.

The Spaniards told Pike that, as soon as Dr. Robinson arrived in Santa Fe, he was taken into custody. He was an American spy, wasn't he? Pike told the soldiers that he and his men were not spies. They were exploring United States territory and had simply gotten lost. Pike told the soldiers that if he had a proper interpreter he could explain the purpose of his expedition as clearly as possible. The soldiers left for Santa Fe, promising to return soon.

On February 26, a hundred Spanish mounted soldiers arrived at the stockade. The commanding officer began by offering to escort Pike from Santa Fe to the Red River.

"What?" replied Pike. "Is this not the Red River?"

"No, sir!" the commander replied, "the Rio del Norte [Rio Grande]."

For the first time, Pike was informed that he was camped along the Rio Grande, and that he was clearly in Spanish territory. The Spanish commander politely pressed his "invitation" for Pike to accompany him to Santa Fe. The province's governor wished to hear an account of the expedition from Captain Pike himself.

*A Mexican cowboy, by Western artist Frederic Remington*

Pike went willingly with the Spanish soldiers. The two groups left the very next day, the Americans traveling on horseback for the first time in many weeks. The route took them due south, and almost at once they felt the change in climate. The snow had melted and wildflowers were starting to appear among the prairie grass.

The Spaniards treated Pike and his men well. They stopped at various mission settlements along the way and were given chocolate, coffee, wine, and various Spanish dishes by local priests. Everywhere they went, people turned out to stare at the Americans, who truly looked like savages from a strange land. They had long beards and matted hair, and only a few even wore shoes.

The men were escorted to the Palace Square, where they stopped at the door of the governor's house. Lieutenant Pike was told to go inside and was quickly admitted to the governor's chamber. Governor Allencaster wasted no time getting right to business: What were Pike's men doing in Spanish territory?

The governor listened intently as Pike described his mission's objectives and explained how they had gotten off course. Pike told the governor there were fifteen men in his party. Then the governor asked if Dr. Robinson had been one of them. Pike, hoping to protect Robinson, said no. The governor, having already been told by Robinson himself that he was part of Pike's expedition, decided that Pike's lie meant he was indeed a spy.

Governor Allencaster allowed Pike to settle in a room but told him to return later with his papers, which the governor wished to look over. Pike had guarded his letters and journal carefully since leaving

*A street scene in Santa Fe, New Mexico*

the stockade and had given some of the papers to each of his men. His trunk contained few of his writings, and he obediently showed those to the governor.

Pike thought all was in order and that he would soon be released. When he heard, however, that outside the governor's house the townspeople were giving liquor to his men, he became alarmed. Pike asked to see his men and then had them turn his papers back over to him. Pike returned all the papers to his trunk—which was then promptly seized by the Spanish.

The papers convinced the governor that Pike was indeed a spy, and he prepared to send the Americans to Chihuahua, in Mexico, for further questioning. The seven Americans, accompanied by many Spanish soldiers, left for Chihuahua on March 4. Pike was ordered not to take any notes as he traveled.

One of the first stops was Albuquerque, where the group visited the commandant of the region. When Pike entered the house, he got a surprise: there was Dr. Robinson "sitting by the fire reading a book"! Although Robinson, too, was considered a political prisoner, his services as a doctor were badly needed and so he had been allowed to practice medicine. Now, though, he was to go along with Pike to Chihuahua.

The rest of the trip was anything but dull. As they stopped at villages along the way, Pike's men were able to talk with whomever they wanted. They were entertained by officials with balls and banquets and greeted by the prettiest girls in the region.

Chihuahua seemed a magnificent place. It was the capital of the Biscay Province and had a number of fine public buildings. They were greeted there by Governor Don Nimesio Salcedo, who had been the last Spanish governor of Louisiana. He told Pike he would have to stay in Mexico until his papers could be thoroughly studied.

Pike was extremely well treated. He could hardly be called a prisoner, even though he was not free to leave. He was entertained by high officials, even the governor, and found the Spanish very hospitable.

Governor Salcedo also decided the papers proved Pike was guilty of spying. However, he did not wish to upset the Americans or risk war, so he decided to return Pike to his country with a strongly worded

*Secretary of State James Madison*

protest to the American government. The governor said he could have—should have—treated Pike and Robinson as common spies.

The American secretary of state, James Madison, replied to the Spanish ambassador that "this government never employed a spy for any purpose." This answer upset the Spanish, who soon cut off diplomatic relations with the United States.

What should we make of this episode? Was Pike on a spying mission? If so, for whom was he spying? General Wilkinson? President Jefferson? Many historians have guessed at Pike's reasons for straying into Spanish territory, but his motives remain unclear.

Lieutenant Pike and his men, in the meantime, were escorted to San Antonio and from there traveled to Natchitoches, Louisiana, a journey that took about two weeks. On July 1, 1807, Zebulon Pike returned home. He had been gone for more than a year.

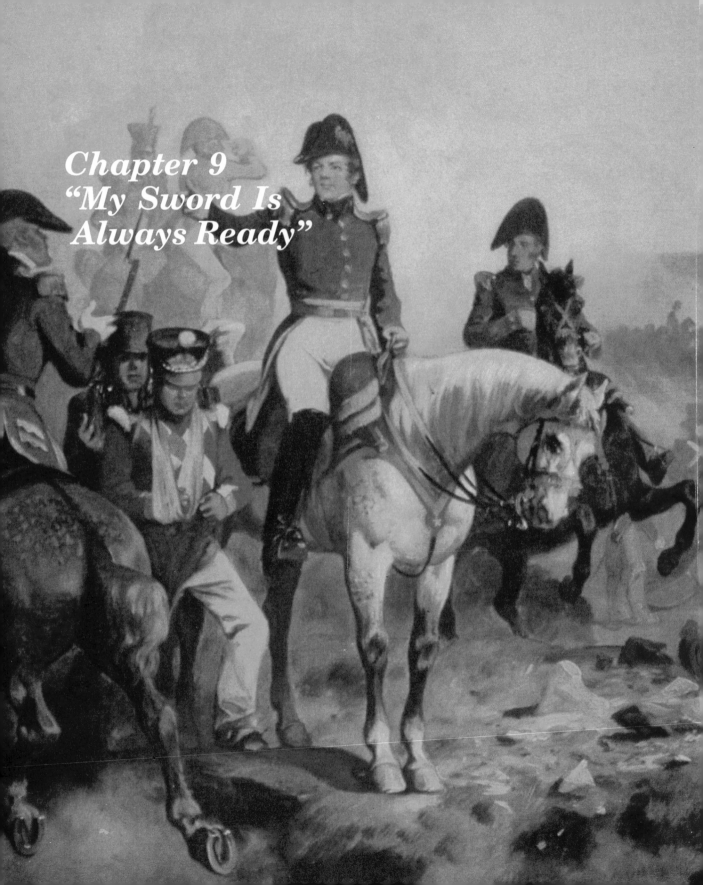

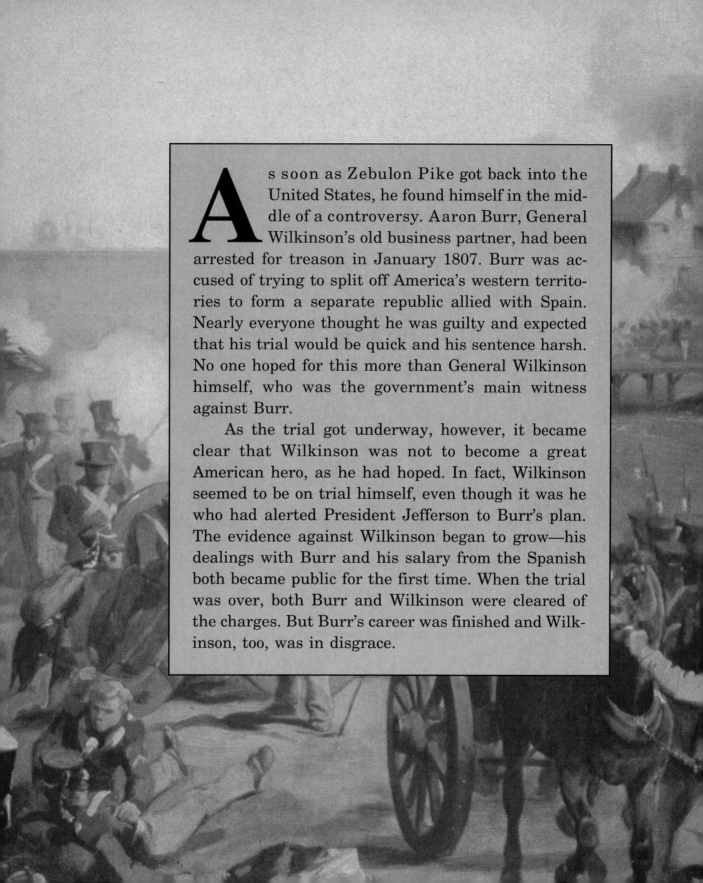

As soon as Zebulon Pike got back into the United States, he found himself in the middle of a controversy. Aaron Burr, General Wilkinson's old business partner, had been arrested for treason in January 1807. Burr was accused of trying to split off America's western territories to form a separate republic allied with Spain. Nearly everyone thought he was guilty and expected that his trial would be quick and his sentence harsh. No one hoped for this more than General Wilkinson himself, who was the government's main witness against Burr.

As the trial got underway, however, it became clear that Wilkinson was not to become a great American hero, as he had hoped. In fact, Wilkinson seemed to be on trial himself, even though it was he who had alerted President Jefferson to Burr's plan. The evidence against Wilkinson began to grow—his dealings with Burr and his salary from the Spanish both became public for the first time. When the trial was over, both Burr and Wilkinson were cleared of the charges. But Burr's career was finished and Wilkinson, too, was in disgrace.

When Zebulon Pike returned from the Southwest, many were immediately suspicious of him, too. Hadn't the general, after all, sent Pike on the mission? Had Pike really gotten lost, or did he stray into Spanish territory on purpose? And if he was there on purpose, what was he supposed to be doing? There is evidence to support the idea that Pike and his men were spying for General Wilkinson. But there is just as much proof that he was in the West doing exactly as ordered—namely, trying to bring peace to the Plains Indians, exploring the headwaters of the Arkansas River, and looking for the source of the Red River.

Despite the unanswered questions about Pike's friendship with General Wilkinson, there was complete agreement that he performed his duties with bravery and daring. His accomplishments made him famous throughout the world. This time anyway, the explorer was able to bask in the limelight—at least for a little while.

Clarissa Pike and their daughter, Clara, reached Natchitoches just before Zebulon arrived there from Mexico. After a joyous reunion and a few weeks of rest and medical care, Pike and his family headed to Washington, D.C.

The capital city was an exciting place—especially now that talk of war was in the air. The United States was squabbling with England over shipping rights, and many in Congress wanted to build a strong defense. Political and military men from around the country were coming to Washington to seek positions in the new, larger army.

While in Washington, Captain Pike (he had received a promotion since his return) made full reports to the War Department on his expedition. He twice

visited President Jefferson at the White House and received the president's permission to have his journals published for all the world to read. He met with the secretary of war, General Dearborn. To Pike's great disappointment, however, General Dearborn turned down his request for an army command.

Pike, quickly promoted to major, was instead put in charge of a battalion headed for New Orleans. He had wanted a more important position but was confident that, if a war did come, he could advance quickly. New Orleans, he knew, was very important to the United States. Because of its position at the mouth of the Mississippi, it would be a severe blow to the British to lose shipping rights to the port.

*Above: Fort Dearborn, in northeastern Illinois near Lake Michigan, named after General Henry Dearborn*
*Below: General Henry Dearborn, who served as secretary of war from 1801 to 1809*

Major Pike and his family sailed for New Orleans in January 1809. He spent the next three years performing many duties all over the South. When war with England began in the summer of 1812, Major Pike was one of the most experienced officers in the army. He was more than ready for an important leadership position.

Early in 1812, Pike—now promoted to lieutenant colonel—left New Orleans for Philadelphia. He carried a letter of introduction to President Madison from Louisiana's governor. He was promoted to full colonel on July 6, 1812, just two weeks after the United States had declared war on Great Britain. This war came to be known as the War of 1812.

*The British attack on Washington, D.C., in the War of 1812*

*General William Hull and his troops during the War of 1812*

Colonel Pike's regiment was to serve in the Montreal campaign under General Dearborn. By the end of the summer of 1812, Pike was in charge of seven hundred men. They were young and frightened—most had never fired a gun in their lives.

America's first invasion against British forces in Canada began on July 12, 1812, when General William Hull crossed the river from Detroit, Michigan, into Ontario. His invasion failed, and on August 16 he surrendered Detroit. It was a humiliating defeat for the Americans.

In the fall, Colonel Pike's regiment marched from Albany, New York, to Plattsburg. From this position along Lake Champlain, they would soon advance toward Montreal, some sixty miles (ninety-six kilometers) to the north.

*Oliver Hazard Perry's defeat of the British in the Battle of Lake Erie was a major American victory in the War of 1812.*

In mid-November the troops crossed into Quebec Province, where they met a small force of Canadian and Indian troops. A few shots were fired and the enemy retreated. Pike then burned the Canadian barracks and ordered the troops back to Lake Champlain before attacking again.

Yet the day after Pike's troops returned to Champlain, General Dearborn ordered all regiments back to Plattsburg. Colonel Pike was stunned. There seemed to be no good reason for a retreat, especially when his campaign had started so promisingly. Yet Pike obeyed the orders of his superior.

The results of General Dearborn's decision were disastrous. The entire invasion now had to be put off until spring, and the troops had to stay in Plattsburg

*York, now Toronto, Canada*

for the winter. They began to build long barracks in late November but did not complete them until Christmas. In the meantime, soldiers had to sleep on the frozen ground, protected only by thin blankets and pine boughs. Hundreds died from exposure.

Many officers left Plattsburg to visit their homes and families. Pike was one of two to remain, and his wife joined him. The soldiers' morale was dangerously low. There were brawls, riots, and murders.

Colonel Pike tried to maintain discipline in his regiment, and generally succeeded. When spring arrived and plans for an invasion were underway again, Pike's regiment was a model fighting force. In March they headed north again. This time their destination was York, a city we now know as Toronto.

*A sailor being impressed, or drafted, into service in the navy*

Before heading into Canada, Pike was overjoyed to hear of his promotion to brigadier general. General Pike now was able to work out the plan for the Battle of York himself. He knew the Americans badly needed a victory, and he was confident he could deliver it. He decided to cross Lake Ontario and attack York as soon as the ice broke.

By mid-April, the lake was free of ice. Pike decided the unit would set sail on April 23. The night before battle, Pike wrote several letters to his family, including one to his father, saying: ". . . if success attends my steps, honor and glory await my name— if defeat, still shall it be said we died like brave men and conferred honor even in death on America."

The landing went perfectly. As the troops pushed into York they overran enemy batteries one after another. The American ships offshore concentrated their fire upon the fort that guarded the town. Pike and his men had, in the meantime, advanced to within 400 yards (366 meters) of the fort.

The British commander saw that his situation was hopeless and raised a white flag. Pike sent one of his men forward to find out if the British would agree to a formal surrender. The general then gathered the rest of his men around him to discuss the fighting and await word.

*The British burn their ships after the capture of York.*

Suddenly, there was a terrible explosion. An abandoned British ammunition storehouse had blown up, scattering rocks and debris in every direction. When the dust cleared, Pike was lying on the ground. He'd been badly wounded in the back and was losing blood fast. His men knew there was no hope.

Pike was quickly taken to one of the navy ships waiting in the harbor. As he lay dying, he could hear the shouts of victory from his men on shore. He smiled at the thought that York was his. He told his grieving men, "Push on my brave fellows . . . ," then he died.

General Zebulon Pike was only thirty-four years old at the time of his death. He had led two important army expeditions into unmapped wilderness and had now carried out a brilliant military victory. In his short life he had surely brought honor and glory to his name—or had he?

Zebulon Montgomery Pike was a good, honest man. He wanted desperately to win the fame and respect that Meriwether Lewis and William Clark had enjoyed at the end of their expedition into the northwest territories in 1806. Pike believed his travels were just as significant to all Americans. What's more, the hardships he and his men had suffered were even greater than those endured by Lewis and Clark. Yet Lewis and Clark have claimed an important place in American history, while Pike's explorations seem minor in comparison.

Part of the reason is Pike's unceasing loyalty to General Wilkinson, who to this day is considered, along with Aaron Burr, one of America's worst traitors. It seems that Pike always saw Wilkinson through the eyes of a boy and was never able to see the older man's obvious faults. Also, Pike could never quite

*Zebulon Montgomery Pike, soldier and adventurer, who died in 1813 at the age of thirty-four*

make up for his lack of formal education. The far more interesting writings of Lewis and Clark were more widely read and admired than the somewhat awkward journals of Pike.

Still, Zebulon Pike's contributions to the winning of the American West were great. He helped the American public see the immense importance of the Western lands. Americans now knew that the West was not just for special interests—in other words, not just for trade and commerce. Instead, the vast lands between the Mississippi and the Pacific Ocean were of the greatest importance for the future of all the nation's people. Winning control of these lands, America's leaders now realized, was a challenge worthy of their best efforts.

*Appendices*

## Pike's Sighting of the Peak

Zebulon Pike first saw the mountain now called Pikes Peak (left) on November 15, 1806. On that day, he wrote in his journal:

15th November, Saturday.—Marched early. Passed two deep creeks and many high points of the rocks; also, large herds of buffalo. At two o'clock in the afternoon I thought I could distinguish a mountain to our right, which appeared like a small blue cloud; viewed it with the spy glass. . . . When our small party arrived on the hill they with one accord gave three cheers to the Mexican mountains. Their appearance can easily be imagined by those who have crossed the Allegheny; but their sides were whiter as if covered with snow, or a white stone. . . . They appear to present a natural boundary between the province of Louisiana and New Mexico and would be a defined and natural boundary. . . .

On November 27, 1806, when Pike finally reached the top of Cheyenne Mountain and saw the peak in the distance, he wrote:

The thermometer which stood at 9 degrees above 0 at the foot of the mountain, here fell to 4 degrees below 0. The summit of the Grand Peak, which was entirely bare of vegetation and covered with snow, now appeared at the distance of 15 or 16 miles from us, and as high again as what we had ascended, and would have taken a whole day's march to have arrived at its base, when I believe no human being could have ascended to its pinical. This with the condition of my soldiers who had only light overalls on, and no stockings, and every way ill provided to endure the inclemency of the region. . . .

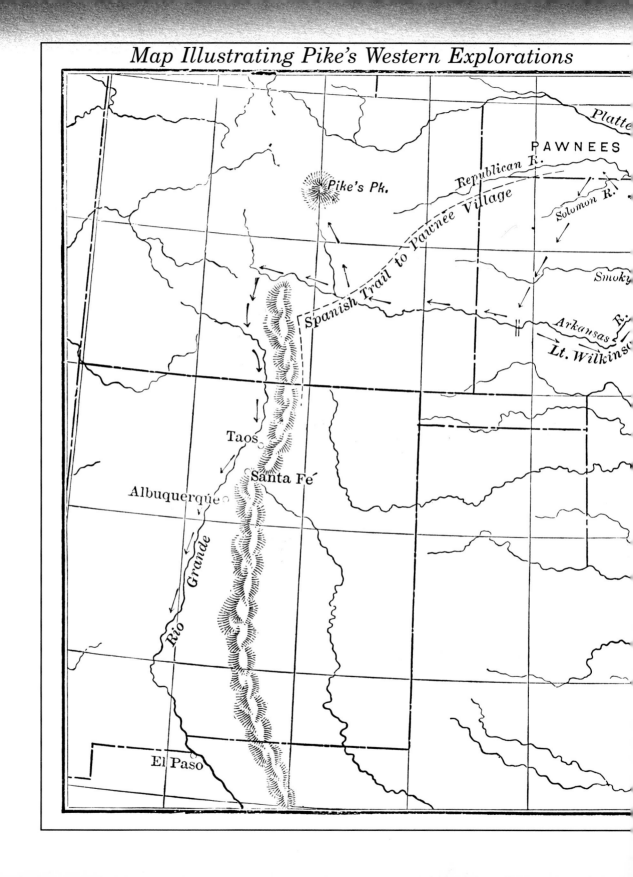

# Map Illustrating Pike's Western Explorations

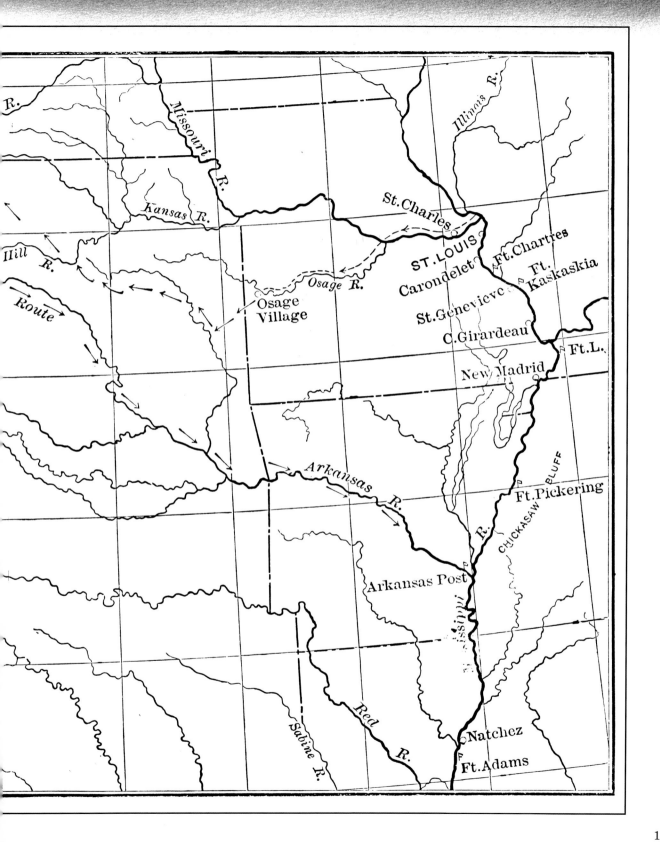

## Wilderness Animals

Pike encountered many different kinds of animals on his explorations. Here are some of his descriptions of animals:

January 31, 1806—Saw a very large animal, which, from its leaps, I supposed to have been a panther; but if so, it was twice as large as those on the lower Mississippi.

August 5, 1806—Today in our tour I passed over a remarkably large rattlesnake, as he lay curled up, and trod so near him as to touch him with my foot, he drawing himself up to make room for my heel. . . . I then turned round and touched him with my ram-rod, but he showed no disposition to bite, and appeared quite peaceable. The gratitude which I felt towards him for not having bit me induced me to save his life.

September 6, 1806—In the holes in the creek we discovered many fish, which, from the stripes on the bellies, and their spots, I supposed to be trout and bass; they were twelve inches long.

October 24, 1806—The wishtonwish [prairie dogs] reside on the prairies of Louisiana in towns or villages. . . . Their residence, being underground, is burrowed out. . . . Their holes descend in a spiral form, therefore I could never ascertain their depth. . . .

December 1, 1806—The difficulty of procuring food rendered [the magpies] so bold as to light on our men's arms and eat meat out of their hands.

December 25, 1806—Caught a bird of a new species, having made a trap for him. This bird was of a green color, almost the size of a quail, and had a small tuft on its head like a pheasant, and was of the carnivorous species; it differed from any bird we ever saw in the United States.

## Wilderness Food

Here are some of Pike's food notes:

December 25, 1805—Gave out two pounds of extra meat [and] two pounds of extra flour . . . in order to distinguish Christmas day.

January 19, 1806—While at this post I eat roasted beavers. . . . it was excellent. . . . I also eat boiled moose's head, which when well boiled, I consider equal to the tail of the beaver; in taste and substance they are much alike.

February 1, 1806—Had a good dish of coffee, biscuit, butter, and cheese for supper.

August 20, 1806—When the council was over we . . . halted at the quarters of the chief, where we were regaled with boiled pumpkins. . . .

October 16, 1806—Killed two more buffalo . . . and feasted sumptuously on the marrow-bones.

October 24, 1806—We found [prairie dogs] excellent meat, after they were exposed a night or two to the frost, by which means the rankness acquired by their subterraneous dwelling is corrected.

November 27, 1806—It began to snow, and we sought shelter under the side of a projecting rock, where we, all four, made a meal on one partridge and a piece of deer's ribs the ravens had left us, being the first we had eaten in that 48 hours.

December 24, 1806—We . . . found ourselves all assembled together on Christmas Eve, and appeared generally to be content, although all the refreshment we had to celebrate that day with, was buffalo meat, without salt, or any other thing whatever.

February 26, 1807—We first breakfasted on some deer, meal, goose, and some biscuit. . .

# Timeline of Events in Pike's Lifetime

1779—Zebulon Montgomery Pike is born near Lamington, New Jersey

1781—American Revolutionary War ends

1792—General Anthony Wayne takes command of troops protecting the western frontier

1794—Pike enlists in the army; American troops defeat Indians in the Battle of Fallen Timbers

1795—Indians sign the Treaty of Greenville, giving up their lands in Ohio and eastern Indiana territories; Pike is assigned to Fort Massac on the Ohio River to inspect barges and halt illegal river traffic

1799—Pike is promoted to second lieutenant and, later, first lieutenant

1801—Pike marries Clarissa Brown of Sugar Grove, Kentucky

1802—Pike and Clarissa move to Fort Knox on the Wabash River at Vincennes

1803—In the Louisiana Purchase, the United States buys Louisiana territory from the French; Pike is transferred to Fort Kaskaskia, on the Mississippi River south of St. Louis

1804—Congress divides Louisiana Territory into two sections, Upper Louisiana and the Territory of Orleans; Meriwether Lewis and William Clark begin their Northwest expedition

1805—James Wilkinson becomes governor of Upper Louisiana; he commissions Pike to make an expedition up the Mississippi River to its source; Aaron Burr kills Alexander Hamilton in a duel

1806—Pike returns from his Upper Mississippi River expedition; Lewis and Clark return from their expedition into the Northwest; Wilkinson sends Lieutenant Pike on a western expedition to the Rocky Mountains

1807—Pike is taken custody by the Spanish on suspicion of being a spy; he is released, returns to the United States, and is promoted to captain

1809—Pike, promoted to major, is stationed in New Orleans

1812—Now a colonel, Pike joins in the War of 1812, serving under General Dearborn

1813—Pike is killed in the Battle of York

# Glossary of Terms

**agent**—An official representative of a government; term also refers to a spy

**apprentice**—A person who learns a skill by serving a master worker

**barge**—A flat-bottomed boat for transporting goods on rivers

**battery**—An army unit of artillerymen, or gun-bearing soldiers

**cargo**—Transported goods

**casualties**—People wounded or killed in battle

**channel**—A narrow stream of water between two bodies of land

**clapboard**—Narrow board used for siding on a house, with one edge usually wider than the other

**continent**—One of the seven large landmasses on the earth

**controversy**—A dispute among people with opposite views

**council**—A meeting for discussion

**drill**—An exercise for training soldiers to march and use weapons

**elope**—To run away secretly and get married

**expedition**—A journey taken for a specific purpose

**filibusterer**—A military adventurer who tries to stir up trouble in another country

**frontier**—The region beyond a country's developed, well-settled areas

**informant**—Someone who supplies information to others

**interpreter**—Someone who translates for people who speak different languages

**intimidate**—To make threats or try to frighten

**keelboat**—A shallow, covered riverboat used to carry cargo

**latitude**—Imaginary east-west lines around the earth, parallel to the equator

**migration**—Movement from one country or region to another

**military intelligence**—Secret information about a country's military plans

**militia**—Local armed forces that may be called upon to serve in an emergency

**opportunist**—Someone who tries to use a situation for his or her own advantage

**predicament**—A difficult situation

**rapids**—Part of a river where the current is fast and there are rocks or other obstacles

**recruit**—To bring new members into a group or organization

**scoundrel**—A mean or dishonest person

**shoal**—A shallow place in the water, caused by a bank or sandbar

**stockade**—A row of posts forming a fort or other safe enclosure

**stranded**—Left in a strange place with no way to get out

**supplement**—To add to or increase

**tariff**—A tax on imported or exported goods

**wheeler-dealer**—A crafty or tricky business person

# Bibliography

**For further reading, see:**

Goetzmann, William H. *Exploration and Empire: The Explorer and the Scientist in the Winning of the American West*. Alfred H. Knopf. NY: 1966.

Hollon, W. Eugene. *The Lost Pathfinder: Zebulon Montgomery Pike*. University of Oklahoma Press. Norman, OK: 1949.

Jackson, Donald, ed. *The Journals of Zebulon Montgomery Pike*. 2 vols., with related letters and documents. University of Oklahoma Press. Norman, OK: 1966.

Pike, Zebulon Montgomery. *Sources of the Mississippi and the Western Louisiana Territory*. Reprint of 1810 edition. March of America Facsimile Series, vol. 57. University Microfilms, Inc. Ann Arbor, MI: 1966.

Terrell, John Upton. *Zebulon Pike: The Life and Times of an Adventurer*. Weybright and Talley. NY: 1968.

# Index

**Page numbers in boldface type indicate illustrations.**

## Picture Identifications for Chapter Opening Spreads

6-7—The Great Plains of the American West

16-17—Raising the Liberty Pole during the American Revolution

24-25—Farming settlement in the Midwest

36-37—Part of the vast lands of the Louisiana Purchase

46-47—The Mississippi River

60-61—Lake Itasca, the true source of the Mississippi River

74-75—New Mexico

88-89—The Rocky Mountains

102-103—The Battle of Plattsburg in the War of 1812

## Acknowledgement

For a critical reading of the manuscript, our thanks to John Parker, Ph.D., Curator, James Ford Bell Library, University of Minnesota, Minneapolis, Minnesota.

## Picture Acknowledgments

THE BETTMANN ARCHIVE: 8, 10, 31, 59, 77, 106, 113

© CAMERAMANN INTERNATIONAL, LTD: 15, 60-61, 88-89

© JERRY HENNEN: 5, 6-7, 12, 46-47, 82, 93

© VIRGINIA GRIMES: 87

HISTORICAL PICTURES SERVICE, CHICAGO: 2, 4, 16-17, 19, 21, 22, 27, 30, 41, 51, 53, 54, 69, 71, 73, 111

JIG: © BETTY GROSKIN, 36-37; © SAM SAYLOR, 86

JOURNALISM SERVICES: 35

NORTH WIND PICTURE ARCHIVES: 13, 20, 23, 26, 29, 33, 39, 43, 45, 8, 50, 55, 63, 64, 65, 66, 68, 79, 83, 90, 91, 92, 96, 97, 99, 101, 105 (2 photos), 107, 109, 110, 116-117

PHOTRI: 85; © MARK S. MYERS, 9

H. ARMSTRONG ROBERTS: 11, 18, 56, 57, 67, 78, 80, 114

© JAMES P. ROWAN: 28, 38, 81

SHOSTAL ASSOCIATES/SUPERSTOCK INTERNATIONAL, INC.: 74-75

TOM STACK & ASSOCIATES: © KEVIN MAGEE, 72

SUPERSTOCK INTERNATIONAL, INC.: 102-103, 108

TSW-CLICK/CHICAGO: © PATRICIA THRASH, 24-25; © TOM TILL, 94

UPI/BETTMANN NEWSPHOTOS: 44

COVER ILLUSTRATION BY STEVEN GASTON DOBSON

## About the Author

Susan Sinnott began her publishing career as an editor for *Cricket*, a children's magazine. She later worked at the University of Wisconsin Press, where she managed and edited academic journals. Eventually, her own two children pulled her away from the scholarly world and helped her to rediscover the joys of reading, writing, and editing books for young readers. Ms. Sinnott now lives in a rattly old house in Portsmouth, New Hampshire, where she is lucky enough to be able to sit at her desk and look out at the lovely harbor. When she's not writing or reading or looking out the window, she's usually caught in the middle of a swarm of kids.